# The Pilgrims

R. Conrad Stein

CHILDRENS PRESS®
CHICAGO

**Library of Congress Cataloging-in-Publication Data**

Stein, R. Conrad.
  The pilgrims / by R. Conrad Stein.
    p. cm. – (Cornerstones of freedom)
  ISBN 0-516-06628-5
  1. Pilgrims (New Plymouth Colony)—Juvenile literature.
2. Massachusetts—History—New Plymouth, 1620-1691—
Juvenile literature.  3. Massachusetts—Social life and
customs—To 1775—Juvenile literature.  [1. Pilgrims
(New Plymouth Colony)  2. Massachusetts—History—
New Plymouth, 1620-1691.]  I. Title.  II. Series.
F68.S887   1995
974.4'8202 – dc20                              95-3292
                                                  CIP
                                                  AC

©1995 by Childrens Press®, Inc.

They were called "Puritans" because they hoped to restore Christianity to its "ancient purity." The Puritans, who originated in England during the early 1500s, rejected grand churches with towering domes. They believed in a simple life and in the power of prayer. Eventually, the Puritans gained influence over the Church of England. But the success of the Puritan movement angered some Puritans who held especially strict Christian beliefs. Some broke away from the main group of Puritans. Those who chose to separate themselves from the rest of the Puritans were called "Separatists."

*The Pilgrims preparing to leave Europe*

*Captain John Smith*

One band of Separatists rose in the village of Scrooby, England. Seeking religious freedom, they moved to Holland in 1608. After a dozen years, they grew tired of Holland and decided to move again—this time to America.

*America!* The vast land across the Atlantic Ocean had long excited the English. They viewed it as a place full of danger, but one that promised new beginnings for those with the courage to emigrate. Twice in the late 1500s, British people had attempted to establish colonies on Roanoke Island off the coast of present-day North Carolina. The first successful English settlement began in 1607, when a band of about one hundred colonists, led by Captain John Smith, founded Jamestown in what is now Virginia.

*The colony of Jamestown*

In July 1620, the Scrooby Separatists assembled in England to make final plans for the daring venture. They received money for their American voyage from a group of London investors. The investors hoped to be paid back with shipments of fish, furs, and lumber from the New World.

One of the Scrooby Separatists was William Bradford, who later became the group's leader. Bradford wrote that the people were fearful before the journey, "but they knew they were Pilgrims and...[lifted] their eyes to the heavens, their dearest country, and quieted their spirits." That one sentence was the only reference Bradford or any of the other Separatists made to the word "Pilgrim." A pilgrim is a person who undertakes a journey for religious purposes. History has since called the Scrooby Separatists the "Pilgrims" because they journeyed to America, hoping to find the freedom to worship as they pleased.

*William Bradford*

*The Pilgrims depart for the New World.*

In England, the Pilgrims were joined by another group of colonists eager to go to America. These people were not on a holy mission. They were farmers and tradesmen who wanted to find a better life in the new land. The Pilgrims were displeased with the addition of the new group, but the London financial backers insisted that they be included. The Pilgrims called the group the "Strangers"; they referred to themselves, the God-fearing travelers, as the "Saints."

The Saints and Strangers boarded two ships, but one ship leaked so badly it had to be left behind in the town of Plymouth, England.

The party of 102 passengers was then forced to crowd onto the remaining vessel, the *Mayflower*. On September 16, 1620, the *Mayflower* sailed from Plymouth into the pages of history.

The Atlantic crossing was a nightmare. The passengers had to cope with horrible overcrowding. If placed on a football field, the *Mayflower* would extend from the end zone at its stern to the thirty-yard line at its bow. Its width was considerably less than that of a football field. In these cramped quarters, the people prepared food, ate, slept, and went to the bathroom. Those who became seasick vomited, sometimes on their neighbors. In a matter of days, the ship was filled with a terrible stench.

*A modern reconstruction of the* Mayflower *shows the ship's cramped sleeping quarters.*

Midway into the crossing, the *Mayflower* ran into a storm that tossed it about like a toy boat in a bathtub. Screaming winds threatened to tear the masts from the deck. The passengers shivered below decks, wondering if the ship would be toppled by the gigantic waves. They huddled together and chanted prayers.

*Opposite page: The* Mayflower *at sea*

At dawn on November 19, 1620, a crewman shouted, "Land!" Everyone rushed on deck. Many miles away, barely visible on the horizon, they could see a strip of shoreline. The Puritans dropped to their knees and thanked God for delivering them to the New World. The voyage had lasted sixty-six days and nights. During that time, one man died and a woman gave birth to a baby, so their total number remained 102.

Cautiously, the ship's captain approached the finger of land known today as Cape Cod, Massachusetts. Arguments then broke out on the ship. The crew of the *Mayflower* wanted simply to discharge the passengers and return to England before the winter storms became worse. Many passengers, especially the Strangers, argued that the *Mayflower* should sail farther south so they could be closer to the British colony at Jamestown. The bickering spread and threatened to doom the mission before it started.

*Miles Standish*

*The Pilgrims sign the Mayflower Compact.*

Sane thinking finally prevailed and saved the enterprise. After a conference, the travelers decided to put aside individual disagreements and pledge full obedience to group decisions. On November 21, they drew up a document, which is today called the Mayflower Compact. It said, "We…solemnly and mutually in the Presence of God…combine ourselves into a civil Body Politick." One of the first to sign the Mayflower Compact was Captain Miles Standish, whom the people recognized as their military leader. He was a Stranger, not a Saint. His signature helped to unify the party. In all, forty-one adult males signed the Mayflower Compact. No women signed the document because in those days, women had few legal rights.

The party's first group decision was to settle in the region where the *Mayflower* had first sighted land. Seeking an agreeable spot, the Pilgrims sent out exploring parties. Scouts traveled on foot and in the longboat that was carried on the deck of the *Mayflower.* One group, under the command of Miles Standish, encountered a band of four or five Indians. After firing some arrows at the Pilgrims, the Indians fled into the forest. Many months would pass before the Pilgrims had any other contact with Native Americans.

*Miles Standish and his first landing party encounter a band of Indians.*

*While the Mayflower sat at anchor, a party in a longboat searched for a proper place for the rest of the Pilgrims to land.*

The men in the longboat continued searching the coastline. They eventually discovered an inviting place with a natural harbor and a brook that provided fresh water. The boatmen might or might not have noticed a ten-ton, granite boulder jutting out of the sand near the beach. Now called "Plymouth Rock," it is one of the most famous historical landmarks in America.

Every day, as the *Mayflower* sat in the harbor at anchor, the temperature dropped. Waves dashed over the crew rowing the longboat, and Bradford claimed that the spray "froze so hard...on their coats that [it looked] as if they had been glassed." After a meeting, the Pilgrims decided to establish a settlement at the place with the harbor and the brook. The *Mayflower* sailed to the spot, and on December 30, 1620, twenty Pilgrims climbed off the ship and stepped onto the soil at Plymouth.

Today, it is difficult to imagine the newcomers' thoughts as they walked inland, looking with wonder at their new home. Probably they felt relief that they had finally arrived, and fear about their desperate circumstances. There were no houses or friendly people to greet them. Perhaps Indians lurked in the woods, waiting for an opportunity to attack. The land looked desolate, even hostile. Snow swirled at the Pilgrims' feet. An icy wind howled in the bare trees. These bleak grounds were now Plymouth Colony—their home, for better or for worse.

*Fierce winter winds made for an unpleasant arrival at Plymouth.*

The first winter was so terrible that many Pilgrims must have believed God had forgotten them. Food was scarce. Disease, probably pneumonia, swept through the settlement. Among people weakened by hunger, the sickness proved to be deadly. Half of the colonists died during that first, bitter winter. Death in such mind-numbing numbers stunned and demoralized the survivors. One of the colonists wrote in his journal, "This month 13 of our numbers die....Of a hundred persons scarce fifty remain, and the living are scarce able to bury the dead."

*A family is given its ration of a handful of corn during the first, painful winter at Plymouth.*

*For years before the Pilgrims arrived, European fur traders had traded with North American Native Americans.*

In addition to being haunted by disease and death, the Pilgrims lived in terror of being attacked by Native Americans. The Pilgrims, like most European settlers of the time, believed the Native-American Indians were heartless savages, beasts who lusted for blood. The Pilgrims were so afraid of Indian attacks that they buried their dead at night. They knew there might be Indian spies watching from the woods, and the Pilgrims wanted to hide the fact that their numbers were dwindling. The Pilgrims did not want their population to appear small enough that they would seem an easy target.

Certainly the Native Americans had many reasons to hate the strangers from Europe. For more than one hundred years, coastal Indians had been in contact with white fishermen and fur traders. Much of the interchange was

Squanto was a Patuxet Indian who once had lived at the site of Plymouth. The story he told of his recent life was wondrous, even bizarre. As a young man, Squanto was kidnapped by English fishermen. They took him to Europe and sold him as a slave in Spain. Squanto escaped from slavery and went to England, where he lived for almost nine years. He eventually returned to North America. Upon his return, Squanto trekked to his old village, only to discover that the plague had wiped out his tribe, and the only survivors had scattered and were living with other tribes. Squanto joined the Wampanoag tribe.

Despite his ordeals, he liked Englishmen. He told the settlers he was willing to teach them how to hunt and to farm the land. To the Pilgrims, his presence was a miracle. William Bradford said of Squanto, "[He was] a special instrument sent of God for [our] good beyond [our] expectations."

In the spring, Squanto taught the Pilgrims how to plant corn, and to put dead herring on top of the seeds. The fish acted as a fertilizer. This Indian method of farming worked wonders in the New England soil. Corn for flour and grapes for wine flourished. Squanto also showed the settlers how to tap into maple trees and extract the sugary sap. A skilled hunter, he helped them shoot the deer and wild turkeys that roamed the woods. Fresh meat appeared in the settlement and buoyed the spirits of the colonists.

*Squanto teaches the Pilgrims how to plant and cultivate crops.*
*He places a dead herring on top of planted seeds. The herring will act*
*as fertilizer and help the seeds grow.*

On April 1, 1621, the chief of the Wampanoag people, the Pilgrims' nearest neighbors, led a party of sixty braves into the settlement. The Pilgrims realized instantly that this was not a hunting party. These were bold-looking warriors. Captain Miles Standish quickly formed his men into ranks, making sure that they displayed their most powerful weapons. But this day, the Wampanoag had come only to talk.

Fortunately, Squanto was on hand to act as an interpreter. After a long discussion, both sides agreed on the terms of a treaty. The Pilgrims and the Wampanoags promised never to steal goods from each other. Most important, each party agreed to come to the aid of the other if either was attacked by a third party. Squanto knew that a rival tribe, the Narragansett, had long threatened the Wampanoag, making them glad to have allies. The treaty was fair for the Wampanoag and for the whites. It ushered in a period of peace between the Pilgrims and their neighbors that lasted more than fifty years.

*The Pilgrims and Native Americans seal their peace treaty.*

In the summer, Pilgrim families began building cabins along the brook that ran through their settlement. During the winter months, all members of the group had lived crowded together in a hastily built "Common House," which offered no more room nor privacy than did the quarters of the *Mayflower*. On high ground near the row of cabins, they made plans to construct a wooden building. It would serve as a fort, in case they were attacked, and as a meetinghouse for Sunday services.

*A modern reconstruction of the fort built by the Pilgrims*

*Modern visitors to Plymouth, Massachusetts, can visit a re-created version of the Plymouth Colony. Far left: An actor portraying a Pilgrim chopping wood. Left: The rebuilt village oven. Bottom: A typical Pilgrim house.*

23

*The first Thanksgiving*

The harvest of 1621 was a frantic, two-week period when the settlers reaped the yield of an entire summer's growing season. The Pilgrims' first harvest was rich beyond their hopes. Observing a long-standing European tradition, the Pilgrims hosted a harvest festival and invited their neighbors. Some ninety Native Americans joined the party, bringing with them five freshly killed deer as a contribution to the meal. Before eating, the Pilgrims offered prayers of thanksgiving for their abundant crops. Then they all feasted on deer meat, cornbread, pumpkins, fish, and geese. Historians are sure that turkey was served as a side dish, not as the main course, on this first Thanksgiving feast.

Two years later, in 1623, William Bradford declared a Thanksgiving Day of prayer and celebration. The celebration spread to other New England settlements, and the holiday eventually became an annual American ritual. In 1863, 240 years after the first Thanksgiving, President Abraham Lincoln proclaimed that the last Thursday of November would be a national Day of Thanksgiving to honor the memory of the Pilgrims. Thanksgiving is now one of the most popular holidays in the United States. Canada has celebrated Thanksgiving in October for many years.

*The Pilgrims were a deeply religious people. On the first Thanksgiving, they gave thanks to God for their survival in their new home.*

*Plymouth Rock (below) is housed inside this monument (right), which stands near the very spot where the Pilgrims first landed.*

In the late 1620s, the Plymouth Colony thrived, but it never became a city. Few ships from England visited Plymouth in the first decade of its existence. It was not until 1630 that ships began carrying new settlers on a regular basis to the surrounding region. Most of the incoming settlers were Puritans. The majority went to colonies in the wilderness. Scores of ships brought colonists to a woodland port that boasted a fine, natural harbor. It was the village of Boston.

Today, Plymouth is still a small town. Because of its rich history, it is famous as a tourist center. Most visitors to Plymouth go first to the celebrated Plymouth Rock. For generations, Americans believed that the Pilgrims stepped on this flat-topped boulder when they disembarked from the *Mayflower* in 1620. But the rock's true significance to the early colony is unknown. The large boulder jutting up on the beach was not mentioned in Plymouth records until 1741, when plans were made to build a wharf leading from the shore to the sea. The planks of the wharf were to cover the boulder. Upon hearing of the plans, a ninety-five-year-old resident named Thomas Faunce began to weep. Mr. Faunce claimed he was told by his father that the Pilgrims stepped onto the great rock when they first landed. The old man's father came to the colony on a ship that arrived shortly after the *Mayflower*, and he knew many of the original inhabitants.

The story told by Thomas Faunce began an American legend. Americans seemed to love the story about the Plymouth Rock. In order to display the rock more prominently, crews moved it several times, and it broke in half during one of the moves. In the early 1800s, visitors chipped pieces to take home as souvenirs. Since 1921, shortly after the three-hundredth anniversary of the landing, Plymouth Rock has rested in its original spot, protected by a white stone canopy. Because of the souvenir hunters, the boulder is now about one-third the size it was when the Pilgrims arrived. Many historians insist that the Pilgrims landed near the rock, but not on its surface, as poets and artists have recorded.

*The Landing of the Pilgrims by Peter F. Rothermell*

It was the poets and the artists who kept the spirit of the Pilgrims alive in the hearts of Americans. For decades, an 1869 engraving, *The Landing of the Pilgrims,* by the artist Peter F. Rothermell, was re-created on the walls of American schools. The dramatic picture shows the Pilgrims in their longboat, struggling against heavy seas to pull the craft to Plymouth Rock. The poet Henry Wadsworth Longfellow added to the Pilgrim drama with his 1858 work *The Courtship of Miles Standish,* a romantic story told in the form of a poem. Perhaps the most frequently recited Pilgrim poem was written in 1826 by a British woman named Felicia Hemans. For more than one hundred years, American schoolchildren were required to stand in their classrooms and recite the lines (left) of Hemans's poem.

While poets and artists romanticized the Pilgrim story, the long-ago colonists lived it day by day and season after season. Seeking freedom of the spirit, they overcame fear, hunger, and rampaging disease. They courageously carved a home out of the forest.

Later generations of Americans honored the Pilgrims because they created a path for all who followed. William Bradford put this sentiment best when, years after the founding of Plymouth, he wrote, "Thus out of small beginnings greater things have been produced by His hand that made all things of nothing, and gives being to all things that are; and as one small candle may light a thousand, so the life here kindled hath shown unto many, yea, in some sort, to our whole nation."

*A present-day view of Plymouth, Massachusetts*

# GLOSSARY

**Church of England** – the established part of the Christian Church in England in the 1500s

**fertilizer** – a substance mixed into the ground to make the soil more fertile (more productive in growing crops)

**Mayflower Compact** – agreement signed by Pilgrims that ended their arguments upon arriving in America

**pilgrim** – a person who journeys to a foreign land, often as part of a religious movement

**Plymouth Rock** – the spot where legend says that Pilgrims first landed in America

*Plymouth Rock*

**puritan** – a person who practices a religious belief strictly and rigorously

**scarlet fever** – a contagious, deadly disease marked by inflammation of the nose and throat, and a red rash

**Separatists** – a group of Puritans who broke off from the main group and left Europe for America

**smallpox** – a contagious, deadly disease marked by pus-filled growths on the skin

**Strangers** – the group of tradesmen who joined the Separatists on their journey to America

*Thanksgiving Day*

**Thanksgiving Day** – modern holiday that commemorates feast shared by Pilgrims and Native Americans after the Pilgrims' first successful harvest in America

# TIMELINE

**1607** Jamestown Colony founded
**1608** Separatists leave England for Holland

*July*
Separatists assemble
in England

**1620**
**1621**
**1623**

William Bradford declares
official Thanksgiving Day

*September 16*
Pilgrims depart for
America on the
*Mayflower*

*November 19*
Pilgrims first
sight land

*November 21*
Mayflower Compact
signed

**1741** First mention of "Plymouth Rock"
in the colony's records

*December 30*
Pilgrims come ashore
at Plymouth

*March*
Samoset and Squanto
visit the Pilgrims

**1863** Thanksgiving Day proclaimed national
holiday by President Lincoln

*April*
Wampanoag Indians and
Pilgrims make treaty

*Autumn*
The Pilgrims'
first, three-day
Thanksgiving feast

**1921**

Plymouth Rock
returned to site of
original Pilgrim landing

**INDEX**  (*Boldface* page numbers indicate illustrations.)

## PHOTO CREDITS

Cover, *The First Sermon Ashore, 1621* by Jean Leon Gerome Ferris. *c.* 1920/Archives of 76; 1, *The Return of the Mayflower, 1621* by J.L.G. Ferris. *c.* 1907/Archives of 76; 2, ©Michele Burgess/SuperStock, Inc.; 3, 4 (top), Bettmann; 4 (bottom), Stock Montage, Inc.; 5, 6, Bettmann; 7, ©Ken Martin/AMSTOCK; 8, Bettmann; 10 (top), North Wind Picture Archives; 10 (bottom), *The Mayflower Compact, 1620* by J.L.G. Ferris. *c.* 1925/Archives of 76; 11, North Wind; 12, *The Mayflower* by W. F. Halsall, 1882/Courtesy of the Pilgrim Society, Plymouth, Massachusetts; 13, Stock Montage, Inc.; 14, 15, North Wind; 17, Bettmann; 19, Stock Montage, Inc.; 20, 21, North Wind; 22, 23 (top right), ©Ken Martin/AMSTOCK; 23 (top left, bottom), ©John Wells/New England Stock Photo; 24, *The First Thanksgiving, 1621* by J.L.G. Ferris. *c.* 1915/Archives of 76; 25, North Wind; 26 (both photos), ©Ken Martin/AMSTOCK; 28, *Landing of the Pilgrims*, an engraving by Peter F. Rothermell/Culver Pictures, Inc.; 29, ©Thomas H. Mitchell/New England Stock Photo; 30 (top), ©Ken Martin/AMSTOCK; 30 (bottom), Archives of 76; 31 (top); 31 (bottom), ©Ken Martin/AMSTOCK

## ADDITIONAL PICTURE IDENTIFICATIONS

Cover: *The first general meeting and religious sermon on shore at Plymouth on January 21, 1621*
Page 1: *After enduring their difficult first winter at Plymouth, the Pilgrims watched as the* Mayflower *returned to England in the spring.*
Page 2: *A monument to the Pilgrims that stands at Plymouth today*
Page 3: *The Pilgrims pray before embarking on their journey across the Atlantic Ocean.*

## EDITORIAL STAFF

Project Editor: Mark Friedman
Design & Electronic Composition: TJS Design
Photo Editor: Jan Izzo
Cornerstones of Freedom Logo: David Cunningham

## ABOUT THE AUTHOR

R. Conrad Stein was born and grew up in Chicago. After serving in the U.S. Marine Corps, he attended the University of Illinois, where he earned a B.A. in history. He later studied in Mexico, where he received an advanced degree in fine arts.

Reading history is Mr. Stein's hobby. He tries to bring the excitement of history to his work. Mr. Stein has published many history books aimed at young readers. He lives in Chicago with his wife and their daughter, Janna.